GWRYCH CASTLE

A Pictorial History

Hesketh Coat of Arms

GWRYCH CASTLE
A Pictorial History

by

Mark Baker

FOREWORD
by
the Chairman of Llanddulas Village Hall Association,
Mrs. Liz Legge.

First published in 2000 by Mark Baker

Printed by
GEE & SON, (DENBIGH) Ltd.,
Chapel Street, Denbigh, North Wales.
PRINTERS, PUBLISHERS & BOOKBINDERS

CONTENTS

Meeting the Prince of Wales in Ruthin, North Wales, March 1999.
His Royal Highness provides much encouragement

FOREWORD

Dear Reader,

The members of Llanddulas Village Hall Association congratulate Mark on his tireless efforts in researching the history of the Dundonald family and their involvement with the Village Hall. Our committee has worked very hard over a number of years to rescue this building from the fate which has befallen Gwrych Castle. This hard work has now been recognised by this book.

We appreciate too the interest and support that Mark has given the Village Hall and we wish him every success with his campaign and future plans.

Yours sincerely,

E. A. Legge

In Loving Memory
of
Those who remain close to my heart,
Maisie Getley, Carl Hammersley, William McLellan (Bill) and Derek Jones (Artist).
For their genuine encouragement and affection.
Also
In Loving Memory
of
Winifred Bamford-Hesketh,
Who loved and cared for Gwrych

Love and thanks always to Mum, Dad, Nan, Grandad, Eric, Pam and all my family.
With special thanks to Peggy and David Jones.

"The Sea is His and He made it:
And His hands prepared the dry land!"

Quoted from the inscription on
Lady Emily's Tower, Gwrych Castle.
Verse 5 : Psalm 95

Mark with Tony Blair, the Prime Minister at No. 10 Downing Street, June 2000.

INTRODUCTION

The origins of this book stem from personal knowledge and research information collected over the last five years. This includes the history of the Hesketh and Dundonald families who lived at Gwrych Castle for the first one hundred and forty years of the Castle's life.

Following numerous requests for a follow-up from the first publication of *The Rise and Fall of Gwrych Castle*, this pictorial portrayal of Gwrych Castle and grounds is intended to commemorate this magnificent Grade One Listed building.

Gwrych, once a romantic dream, housing a luxurious interior, surrounded by a palacious park and spectacular exterior, is now sadly neglected.

If we are to protect buildings of heritage for future generations, I believe that we can make a difference.

The support offered by the supporters of ASFOG has been terrific. In particular, the support of Margaret Lambert Jones (Chair – ASFOG) and Mrs. Doris Thornton, born in Tan yr Ogo Lodge at Gwrych, has been stupendous. I have aimed to raise awareness of the Castle's plight – some photographs are included in the book.

The support of so many, for example the community of Llanddulas and the members of the Village Hall, which has been very encouraging and inspiring.

I hope that you enjoy the book, which is intended to encapsulate the life and times of Gwrych Castle, including photographs of the inhabitants, some of the treasures and the building's unfortunate sad demise.

MARK BAKER
November 2000

HESKY'S OLD LIBRARY, (The Hesketh Family)

A very early lithograph of Gwrych. Circa 1825.

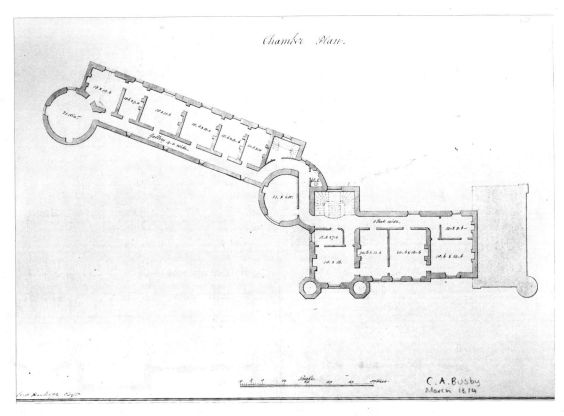

Chamber Plan.

This was a proposed plan for Gwrych by Charles Augustus Busby in 1815.
It was exhibited at the Royal Institute of British Architects. (R.I.B.A.)

14

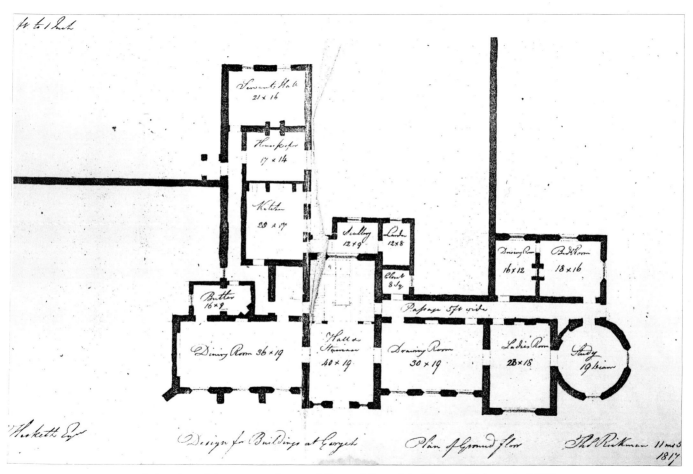

A drawing of the proposed ground floor of Gwrych by Thomas Rickman in 1817.

15

A view from what is now the derelict 'Gwrych Garden Nurseries'.
Drawn by Lloyd Hesketh Bamford-Hesketh. Circa 1820s.

Lloyd Hesketh Bamford Hesketh's view of Gwrych from the south tower. Circa 1820s.

The Formal Gardens which were later the site of the Dance Marquee in the 1950s.
Painted by L. H. Bamford-Hesketh. Circa 1820s.

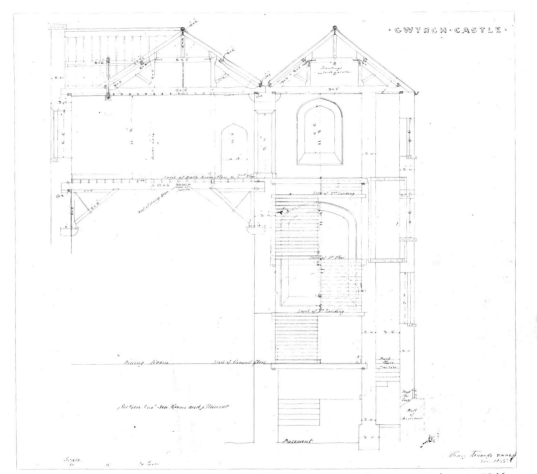

· GWYRCH · CASTLE ·

Henry Kennedy's cantilevered staircase of 1845. This proposed plan was carried out in 1846.

19

The Towers at Gwrych, drawn by Lloyd Hesketh Bamford-Hesketh. Circa 1820s.

Building the outer towers at Gwrych. Circa 1820s.

The exterior of the Stable Block with a gardener at work.
Circa 1820s.

The east front with Lady Emily's Garden Chair. Circa 1820s.

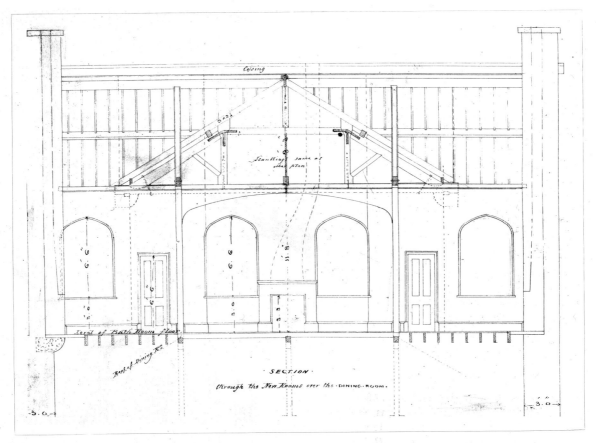

A cross section through the new bedroom axis designed by Henry Kennedy in April 1845.

This beautiful window is in the east end of St. Michael's Church in Abergele. It contains the Hesketh Coat of Arms, 'In Deo mea spes' – In God we trust. The inscription in the window says *'In memory of the Lloyd family now represented by Lloyd H. Bamford-Hesketh, eldest son of Frances Lloyd, heiress of Gwrych'*.

Saint Michael slaying the devil, Saint Michael's Church, Abergele.

THE FORMIDABLE LADY DUNDONALD (Dundonald Family)

The staff of Gwrych in 1890. Some of the staff are buried in St. Cynbryd's Churchyard, Llanddulas.

Workmen at Gwrych in 1912. The Countess commissioned Charles Ernest Elcock to extend Gwrych into an Edwardian Stately Home.

Mr Robert Jones, Gamekeeper at Gwrych. He lived at Nant-y-bella Lodge with his wife and children. He died alone on the Roman steps near his hunting cottage on Cefn Ogof. He fell on his shotgun and was believed to have been found a week later, dead.

Mr Robert Roberts, the Chauffer (far left). Mrs Polly Jones, the maid. The house-keeper, Lady's maid and the Valet

Mr William Jones, of Tan-yr-Ogo Lodge. Father of Doris and Celia.

Mrs Polly Jones of Tan-yr-Ogo Lodge. She was a housekeeper at Gwrych and wife of Mr William Jones.

Robert Roberts of 'the Square', Llanddulas. Chauffer to the Countess of Dundonald. He was sent to London to learn how to drive and eventually taught the Countess herself. Circa 1907.

The Earl and Countess of Dundonald in their car at Gwrych, 1907. The Countess looks suitably miserable due to the fact that she was forced into marriage and didn't like her chosen husband.

The Earl of Dundonald on the Main West Terrace with his Chauffer in circa 1907. The Earl was educated at Eton and was sent directly into the army. He lead the charge at Ladysmith in 1900 and later became a general in the First World War.

Thomas Hesketh Douglas Blair, Lord Cochrane, eldest son of the Earl and Countess at Gwrych in 1907. He was born in Hanover Square, London on the 21st February, 1886. He became the 13th Earl of Dundonald in 1935 and sold Gwrych in 1946.

The Countess of Dundonald opening the Kinmel Manor Garden Fair, August 1910. She is standing next to her best friend, the Archbishop of Wales.

Winifred Bamford-Hesketh, Countess of Dundonald. In her ceremonial robes. She was born in Torquay on the 16th April, 1859 to Robert Bamford-Hesketh and Ellen Bateman-Jones of Pentre Mawr, Abergele. This photograph was taken in 1920, four years before her sudden death.

The Abergele Gates decorated for the home-coming of Lord Dundonald in 1900.

Local celebrations upon Lord Dundonald's arrival from Ladysmith. November, 1900.

Street party preparations to welcome the 'local hero', Lord Dundonald.
New York Terrace, Market Street, Abergele.

Abergele, November 1900.

Looking towards Pensarn, November 1900.

Examples of fine furniture, which were housed in the Castle

Auction Lots 281, 270, 228 from the 1928 sale.
From left to right:
LOT 281: An Antique pair of magnificent cast iron log boxes with unique floral decoration,
each fitted two handles, and on claw feet.
LOT 270: One of six fine old walnut framed chairs, upholstered in hide.
LOT 228: One of six Chippendale chairs.

Lots 142, 272, 269.
From left to right:
LOT 142: A pair of French shield shaped pole screens decorated in enamel and gilt
with tapestry panels.
LOT 272: One of five exquisite Louis Armchairs with gilt mounts, upholstered in figured damask.
LOT 269: A fine Jacobean Oak Chair with an exquisitely carved back.

Lots 197, 198.
From left to right:
LOT **197 & 198**: Two old Buhl envelope card tables, with inlaid decorated enamel tops.

Lots 196,201.

LOT 196: An exquisite Buhl-shaped writing table on four shaped legs with ormolu mounts fitted with three drawers with springs, finely enamelled border, top in inlay and fine shaped green baize panel, 4 ft. 10 in. by 2 ft. 10 in.

LOT 201: Choice French built Mantel clock with Sevrés panels surmounted by figures of cupids and Sevré vase by 'Lépante'.

Lots 191, 200.
From left to right:
LOT 191: An antique Gilt Consol Table with shaped marble slab.
LOT 200: A fine old Buhl plant container inlaid enamelled decoration and ormolu mounts on four cabriole legs.
(Clock Not For Sale!)

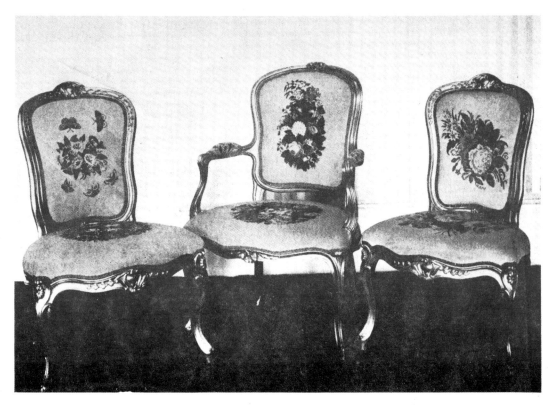

Lot 182.
Three fine Louis gilt single chairs with severed wool-work seats and backs.

The Jewish refugees outside the main door at Gwrych, 1939. The refugees slept in a large tent on the main west terrace and many worked on the Estate. There were two births and one marriage at Gwrych during the time the refugees were there.

Gwrych Newydd, circa 1946. The Gwrych Castle Estate Office. Now the Abergele Grill.

Plas Tan-y-Gopa, circa 1946. It was described as a 'small gentleman's residence'.

A view from Lady Emily's tower overlooking Tan-yr-Ogo. Circa 1946.

The park in between Tan-yr-Ogo and Hen Wrych. Circa 1946.

Hen Wrych from the Hesketh Tower. Circa 1946. Hen Wrych was once the home farm for Gwrych Castle and housed the dairy and the produce garden. The produce garden was where the gardeners would grow vegetables for the Estate.

The Bamford-Hesketh and Dundonald Memorial. This is the burial place for Winifred, Countess of Dundonald, her parents and children. St. Cynbryd's Churchyard, Llanddulas.

Bamford-Hesketh Memorial St. Cynbryd's Church, Llanddulas.

Main Entrance to Gwrych Castle, Abergele. Circa 1950s.

Abergele Gatelodge in the 1930s. It was the first lodge built by Lloyd Hesketh Bamford-Hesketh in the 1820s. The Dutton family have lived in the lodge since 1946.
(Current owners of Gwrych Towers Campsite).

Hen Wrych House. Circa 1946. Hen Wrych dates from the 16th century and was once the home of the famous poet, Felicia Hemans.

Hen Wrych (Old Gwrych) the ancient home of the ancestors of the Castle family 'The Lloyds of Gwrych'. The photograph was taken in 1907.

Plas Tan-yr-Ogo was the home of the widows of Gwrych Castle. Lady Emily Hesketh and her daughter-in-law both lived there when their husband's died. The Hall was built in the 18th Century before Gwrych.

The Tan-yr-Ogo Gate Lodge. Circa. 1960s.

Tan-yr-Ogo Lodge in 1982.

Tan-yr-Ogo Lodge in 1907. The carriage is filled with people who had paid to travel through the park. The proceeds went to the church.

Originally called the Waterloo Towers. Tan-yr-Ogo was built to remember the Battle of Waterloo in 1815. It contains four plaques commemorating the history of the Tan-yr-Ogo pass.

The Tan-yr-Ogo Gate Lodge living quarters. Circa 1920s.

VIEWS OF GWRYCH

An early view of Gwrych from the water tower. Circa 1870s.
This picture was taken before the marble staircase was built.

The west terrace at Gwrych. Circa 1982.

The East Front. Circa 1915.

A spooky photograph of the North Front from about 1935.

A view from the bridge over the A55. Circa 1975.

North Front of Gwrych from Hen Wrych. Circa 1978.

Gwrych Castle, pre 1912.

Gwrych Castle (Seat of Lord Dundonald) // Going for a walk

The East Front in 1903.

A view of Gwrych from the site of the Marquee. Circa 1982.

A romantic view of Gwrych from the park. Circa 1890s.

The Stable Hill and Stable Cafe. Circa 1970s.

A picture of the main front gate of Gwrych. Circa 1946.

The East Front in 1946.

Gwrych from the main West Terrace in 1911.

A painting of Gwrych from the West Terrace in the 1950s. We can see the parasols for the terrace café in the foreground.

Gwrych in 1904. A view from the main West Terrace.

Gwrych from the Abergele Drive, 1940s.

The Castle Garages in Stable Court. Circa 1907.

Gwrych from the Park, 1978.

BEACH, PENSARN.

PROMENADE, PENSARN.

DUNDONALD AVENUE.

GWRYCH CASTLE.

YR ALLT.

ABERGELE

TAN-YR-OGO GATEWAY, GWRYCH CASTLE.

GWRYCH LODGE GATES AND TAN-Y-GOPPA ROAD.

A view of Abergele including three pictures of Gwrych and the gatehouses.

An early view of Gwrych from the hillside looking east.

Gwrych from the Hesketh Tower in 1900 but painted in the 1950s.

A beautiful view of Gwrych from the Hesketh Tower. We can see the visitors to Gwrych on the bank leading up to the castle marvelling at the castle's splendour. Circa 1953.

Bruce Woodcock (boxer) relaxing in the Outer Hall at Gwrych in 1950.

Mr John Graves on the diesel locomotive.
Circa 1950s.

Mr John Graves leaning on the brass balustrade
overlooking the marble staircase.

Randolph Turpin with his father and brother talking to the members of the Rita Landey Choir. They are standing on the base of the marble staircase. Circa 1950.

Two children enjoying their childhood days at Gwrych.

A coach party enjoying a day out at Gwrych. Circa 1953.

Mrs. Graves with Holly the owl at the Castle. Circa 1950s.

Randy Turpin with Holly the owl in 1950.

The Gwrych Castle train. Circa 1950s.

A silver candelabra used in the 1950s at Gwrych.

From left to right:
John Adams, Clementine Adams and Lucy Adams, Summer 1959
whilst staying on holiday at Gwrych.

THE SAD DECLINE

The Outer Hall. Circa 1997.

Ruth Madoc and the owner of the Castle in 1983.

The head of the staircase in 1983.

The staircase looking down. Circa 1990.

The remains of the second floor landing. Circa 1995.

The Marble Staircase in 1980.

The Countess of Dundonald's Fireplace, now gone, in 1997.

The staircase in 1997.

The North Front in 1999.

Johnny Vaughan with Mark on the set of the 'Big Breakfast' (Channel 4), 1998.

Mrs Doris Thornton (neé Jones) of Tan-yr-Ogo Lodge with Mark in April 1998. On the BBC programme 'Country File', she presented a clothing chest to Mark, which originally belonged to the Countess of Dundonald.

From left to right:
Derek Jones (Artist), Mayor of Abergele, Mayor of Rhyl (Mark Jones) and in the centre, Mark Baker. The portrait of the castle was presented to myself in October 1998 in the Mayor's Parlour at Rhyl.

Mr. and Mrs. Jones with Mark Baker at the presentation of the Gwrych Castle portrait, 1998.

William Hague, leader of the Opposition, in North Wales, 1999.

Sebastian Coe and Mark in 1999.

Mark Baker outside the BBC, White City, London, 1999.

Russel Grant and Mark filming at Gwrych, 1999.

CONTACT ORGANISATIONS

Mrs Rosemary Robinson: (Buckinghamshire)

'I have been saddened over the years to witness the deterioration of this historical building. The Castle has such wonderful potential and deserves to be restored to its former glory. First and foremost a revitalisation programme should be put into action to prevent further dilapidation due to the vagaries of the weather to say the least and to the negligence of the local Council'.

Mrs Ivy Eley: (Glan Conwy)

'I last visited Gwrych sixteen years ago, but I always cast a lingering glimpse towards those "magical turrets" when we drive past, en route to Colwyn Bay'.

Michael Salts: (Cumbria)

'Gwrych, though not as ancient as some, is still a valuable part of Welsh heritage and ought to be saved and cared for accordingly. Having the privilege of living there, I am disgusted with the current situation and I want Cadw and the Council to use their powers to restore the building'.

Mr and Mrs Oates: (Yorkshire)

'To see the desecration wrought on the premsies is extremely disturbing, I hope that you can do something to bring it back to what it was!'

Mr Peter A. Rushforth: (Bradford)

'. . . I think the Council should find the cash, because it is a national landmark in the same way that Penrhyn and Bodelwyddan are!'

Mrs Elizabeth Fens (Holland):

'. . . Such a romantic building, it could be restored and used as a centre for children or even as an exhibition place for the books by Enid Blyton, 'The Famous Five', which are just wonderful.'

Mrs Doris Thornton: (Oxfordshire - Born in Tan-yr-Ogo Lodge)

'I do not wish to see the Castle in the state its in. I just want to remember it the way it was . . . I wrote to the Prince of Wales suggesting it would make a wonderful private home for him and his family'.

Although I am too young to understand politics, may I thank all the M.P.'s who have offered support including the Rt. Hon. William Hague and his wife Ffion, for their interest in the Castle and Welsh Heritage.

From the hundreds of individuals who share my concern, it is believed that this situation should never have been allowed to develop. Perhaps the laws to protect the interests of listed buildings are at fault? I believe that it takes just one determined individual to make a difference. The wealth of support which has been forthcoming to A.S.F.O.G. provides much encouragement. Someday soon, we hope to once again walk through those marble halls and take in the rich splendour and majesty of Gwrych Castle.

Mark Baker

As I am continuing to collate information and photographs, I would be most appreciative to receive any details of your memories.

For further information please write to:

Mark Baker - President /Founder A.S.F.O.G. (A Society for the Friends of Gwrych Castle)

c/o 13 Frances Avenue, Rhyl, Denbighshire, North Wales LL18 2LW

ACKNOWLEDGMENTS

TO ALL THOSE WHO HAVE INSPIRED, SUPPORTED AND ENCOURAGED ME

HRH The Prince of Wales
The Prime Minister, Tony Blair
Rt. Hon. William Hague, Leader of the Opposition
Nigel Evans, MP (Patron of ASFOG)
Gareth Thomas, MP
Chris Ruane, MP
Rupert Segar, Presenter BBC 1 Country File
Johnnie Vaughan, Big Breakfast
Kit Martin, Director Phoenix Trust
Manon Williams, Phoenix Trust
Maev Kennedy, Guardian
Caroline McGee, Daily Telegraph
Arieh L. Handler and the Mizarchi Federation, London
Bachad Fellowship, London
Jewish Chronicle, London
John Edelnand, Luton
Miss Dutton
ITV, Channel Four, BBC Wales
Mr Roberts
Harry Thomas
Bob Ellis
Chris Keating
Mike Roberts
Stuart Sandem
Earl of Dundonald (thank you for the portrait photographs!)
Denbighshire and Conwy County Councils
Councillor John Pitt (Patron of ASFOG)

Members of A.S.F.O.G. for their valuable memories
CADW
North Wales Weekly News
Rhyl & Prestatyn Journal and Evening Leader
Gareth Hughes - Daily Post
Siân Wade - Abergele and St. Asaph Visitor
Rhyl, Ruthin, Prestatyn and Abergele Libraries
Beatrice Tunstall
Rosemary A. Robinson
National Library of Wales, Aberystwyth
Royal Institute of British Architects
SAVE Britain's Heritage - Richard Pollard, Secretary
Emily Cole (Commemorative Plaques Historian at English Heritage, London)
Brian Jones
St. Cynbryd's Church, Llanddulas
Doris Thornton
Peggy & David Jones of Rhyl
Idris Davies and the Llanddulas Village Hall supporters
Roberts and Frank Penlington
Staff and pupils of Rydal Penrhos School, Colwyn Bay
Clwyd Books, Siop Ganol, Llanddulas P.O.
WH Smiths, Books Unlimited, Whitesides
With thanks to my family and friends who always support me in everything that I do